Black Power and Post-Colonial Society: Essays on Kwame Ture, Religion, and More

Dwayne Wong (Omowale)

CONTENTS

1 REFLECTIONS ON THE LEGACY OF JOHN LEWIS AND KWAME TURE

The passing of John Lewis on July 17, 2020 offered for me some serious reflection about the nature of the struggle that African people are engaged in. Lewis was a political figure whom I could not help but have a great deal of respect and admiration for, even if I disagreed with some of his tactics and his political positions. I respected Lewis for being someone who was willing to risk his own life to advance the cause of justice, yet I was also very critical of Lewis as well because of the fact that although willingness to risk one's life does display a significant degree of courage, having that type of courage alone is not always the most effective way to bring about the type of change that is truly needed.

Lewis' passing also made me reflect on the legacies of Kwame Ture (formerly Stokely Carmichael) and Jamil Abdullah Al-Amin (formerly H. Rap Brown), who both had served as former chairpersons of the Student Non-Violent Coordinating Committee (SNCC), just as Lewis had done. Unlike Lewis, Ture and Al-Amin had not become part of the political establishment. They risked their lives and suffered just as Lewis had, but they suffered and struggled towards a much different goal. That goal was not to become politicians within the Democratic Party. Ture and Al-Amin had remained opposed to the political establishment.

I reflected on the legacy of Dr. Martin Luther King who could have very well become a member of the political establishment as Lewis had done, but Dr. King decided not to. Instead, Dr. King spoke out against the political establishment. For this reason, he found himself alienated from some of the other leaders in the civil rights movement. Dr. King was just as brave as Lewis and just as willing to risk his life to stand against injustice, but he did so without being drawn into the political establishment.

I also reflected on the legacy of SNCC, which was an organization that had produced some of the most significant civil rights leaders and revolutionary thinkers in America in the 1960s. One of the interesting features about SNCC is that this particular organization represented the differences which existed within the civil rights struggle. In *In Search of African History & Liberation* I wrote about the differences between the nationalists and the integrationists within the movement of the 1960s. SNCC was an organization which contained nationalists such as Ture and integrationists such as Lewis.

Some of the integrationists in SNCC became politicians for the Democratic Party. Marion Barry, the first chairman of SNCC, became the mayor of Washington D.C. John Lewis, who preceded Ture as the chairman of SNCC, was elected to the House of Representatives as a member of the Democratic Party. Julian Bond served as a Democratic member of the Georgia Senate and the Georgia House of Representatives.

Rather than joining the Democratic Party as some of his colleagues in SNCC did, Kwame Ture moved to Guinea where he worked with the government of President Sékou Touré and became an organizer for the All-African People's Revolutionary Party (A-APRP). There seems to be a perception among some that Ture became politically irrelevant in the struggle after he moved to Guinea and began building the A-APRP. For example, an article in the *Workers Vanguard* explained that Kwame Ture and the A-APRP "are totally irrelevant and frequently *obstacles* to today's black struggles." How had the chairman of SNCC who popularized the slogan "Black Power" come to be viewed as someone who was irrelevant to the struggle? Moreover, is this assessment accurate or fair to Ture?

I think Ture's ideas certainly remained very relevant—I share much more of Ture's political ideas than I share Lewis' ideas. Yet, I also understand why some would perceive Ture as having become irrelevant. I am not suggesting that this is an entirely fair assessment because his ideas were relevant and the work that Ture was engaged in was relevant, but the political circumstances which existed in the 1980s and 1990s left Ture isolated within the global Pan-African struggle. Neo-colonialism had subverted the independence movement in Africa and the Black Power movement in the United States had been destroyed.

Ture was forced to wrestle with the contradictions within the movement as well as the pressure that was confronting those who maintained a revolutionary position. Ture remained dedicated to the cause of revolution, but he had become isolated for a number of reasons. In the first place, the Black Power ideology that SNCC began preaching made Ture and others in SNCC targets. H. Rap Brown had explained: "It was obvious when I became Chairman that I was in for trouble. For a year, 'the man' had let Carmichael travel around the country talking about Black Power and 'the man' realized that he had made a serious mistake. He recognized too late that Black people, like the Vietnamese people, were escalating their war of liberation. So it was clear to me that if Black people began to respond by accepting a revolutionary analysis, 'the man' was going to try and silence me."

There indeed was an attempt to silence Brown, who was arrested in 1967. After he was released, Brown explained that he was placed under 24-hour surveillance. He was arrested again in September and placed under house-arrest in New York. Brown was arrested once again for violating bond by attending meetings in California and was jailed yet again. The same type of repression was confronting other black organizations, such as the Black Panther Party and the Republic of New Afrika. Activists were being arrested and jailed, as well as being placed under constant surveillance.

SNCC briefly joined with the Black Panther Party, but this alliance did not work out as effectively as the parties involved would have hoped. Ideological differences emerged between Kwame Ture and the Black Panther Party. Ture's nationalist views prompted public criticism of him from some of the Panthers and from James Forman, who was a member of SNCC as well. In the meanwhile, Rap Brown was facing numerous legal challenges. Ture decided to move to Guinea in 1969. There he also encountered some serious organizational challenges. After Touré died in 1984, Lansana Conté seized power in Guinea and outlawed the Democratic Party of Guinea, which was Touré's party.

By the mid-1980s, Ture lacked a solid political base in Africa for his organizational activities with the A-APRP. He would travel to the United States to give speeches and organize on behalf of the A-APRP, but there was no longer a national mass movement as there had been in the 1960s when Ture first called for Black Power. In Guinea, Ture struggled to help restore the Democratic Party of Guinea back into power, but without any success. This is why I would argue that it would be rather unfair to conclude that the A-APRP was irrelevant and leave the assessment there. Ture encountered some very difficult political challenges, but he remained steadfast in the struggle for the unity and liberation of all African people.

One thing that I have been particularly critical of Kwame Ture for was his support for President Touré's government in Guinea. I understand it. Ture had moved to Guinea where he embraced the revolutionary Pan-African ideology of President Touré. I also understand that there was an ever present need to defend the revolution in Guinea from subversion. There were multiple attempts to overthrow and assassinate Touré, which no doubt contributed to Touré's repressive nature. Ture acknowledged the brutal nature of Guinea's repression against political opponents and critics, but he did not condemn it. He defended it and even argued that Touré was actually too soft. In Ture's view not enough blood had been spilled to protect the revolution in Guinea. Ture's position was clear. The enemy of African people was imperialism and capitalism. Those were the very forces which overthrew Nkrumah and had tried to do the same to Touré. Violent defense of the revolution in Guinea was, in Ture's view, the proper way to handle these destabilization attempts.

I understand the reasons why Ture defended the repressive measures which Touré adopted, but there were two fundamental problems with that approach. The first of which was that the violent repression of counterrevolutionary forces was unchecked, which meant that individuals could be detained and executed merely out of the suspicion that they were engaged in subversive activities. This obviously meant that innocent people were being tortured and killed in the name of protecting the revolution. One of the worst examples of repression was when women in Guinea engaged in mass protests against some of the policies of Touré's government. The government responded by sending the security forces to open fire on the women protesters. In Guinea there was little space for citizens to express legitimate disagreements with the government.

This would remain an issue in Guinea even after Touré's death. Guinea was a military regime under Conté. Moussa Dadis Camara seized power through a coup and also established a brutal military regime. Alpha Condé was elected in 2010, in what seemed to be a return to civilian government after decades of instability and repressive military rule. The problem is that when the people of Guinea engaged in a series of protests against constitutional changes which would allow Condé to seek a third term, Condé did what the prior presidents of Guinea did, which was sending the security forces to violently repress the protests. This included not only opening fire on the protests with live ammunition, which resulted in several deaths, but some of the leaders of the protests against Condé were arrested as well. Ibrahima Diallo and Sékou Koundouno were among those who were detained by the regime in Togo.

A comrade of mine informed me that she had been planning an activity with Diallo and Koundouno in the Gambia before they were abducted. Africans Rising launched a campaign calling for the release of Diallo and Koundouno, which I supported by writing some articles in order to raise awareness to the struggle being waged in Guinea. I mention all of this to make the point that the repression which Touré engaged in would have a long lasting impact on Guinea, but I don't think that Ture himself understood this at the time when he was not only supporting the violent repression which Touré's regime engaged in, but also calling for even more blood to flow.

Such violent repression in the name of defending the revolution also became meaningless given that in the end Touré would adopt a pro-Western position anyway. I pointed out in my book *Africa-Man: A Collection of Pan-African Writings* that Ture found himself in the contradictory position of denouncing imperialism, while defending a government which had been making attempts to reconcile with those same capitalistic Western nations. Perhaps Ture was too attached to the revolution in Guinea to recognize these contradictions or perhaps his admiration for Touré could not allow him to recognize these contradictions. Whatever the case was, there was a clear contradiction between Ture's revolutionary vision and his willingness to support what had become yet another Western backed dictatorship in Africa.

I do not want readers to get the wrong impression. Kwame Ture was a considerable influence in my development as a Pan-Africanist. I especially have drawn a lot from his book *Black*

Power. I have a great deal of admiration for Kwame Ture as a Pan-African revolutionary, but there were contradictory aspects of his politics which troubled me. Despite this, Ture held steadfast to his belief in the Pan-African revolution. He continued in the struggle as a grassroots activist and organizer when some of his colleagues—including John Lewis—decided not to.

One of Ture's great contributions to the struggle against racism in the United States was that his slogan of Black Power clearly articulated that racism was not merely an issue which stemmed from the prejudicial views of white people, but that it was also related to the unequal power relationship as well. He explained racism not only as a form of individual prejudice, but as an entire system. Ture and Charles Hamilton explained in *Black Power*: "Racism is both overt and covert. It takes two, closely related forms: individual whites acting against individual blacks, and acts by the total white community against the black community. We call these individual racism and institutional racism." Institutional racism is more difficult to combat because not only is it covert, but also because individuals tend to internalize institutionalized racism.

Ture and Hamilton also explain: "'Respectable' individuals can absolve themselves from individual blame: *they* would never plant a bomb in a church; *they* would never stone a black family. But they continue to support political officials and institutions that would and do perpetuate institutionally racist policies." Individuals who do not display racist attitudes still contribute to the system of racism by supporting racist institutions and racist political leaders. Racism is not merely a question of prejudice or intolerance towards others who are of a different racial background. It is a question of power.

There were serious contradictions in Ture's political legacy, but was Lewis' legacy any better? Lewis became a member of the Democratic Party, which is a party that has supported dictatorships all over Africa, including the dictatorship in Togo which I had been involved in fighting. The Democratic Party was the party of Bill Clinton, whose criminal justice reforms resulted in a record number of African Americans being incarcerated. The Democratic Party was the party of Barack Obama, who continued America's legacy of misguided military interventions by intervening in Libya's civil war. After Muamar Gaddafi had been killed, Obama gave a speech about supporting this "new Libya." The reality is that Libya fell into civil war and chaos after Gaddafi was toppled. Obama would later admit that his biggest mistake as president was failing to plan for the aftermath of the intervention in Libya. The Democratic Party was also the party which failed to defeat Donald Trump in 2016.

This question of forming an independent political party for African people or joining the Democratic Party were questions that SNCC had been confronting. SNCC had played a role in organizing the Mississippi Freedom Democratic

Party (MFDP) for the purpose of building grassroots political strength among the African masses in Mississippi. The name "Democratic" was included because the MFDP was seeking the recognition of the Democratic Party. The MFDP decided that since African people were excluded from the state Democratic Party then it would select its own delegates to challenge the state party for the right to represent the state. The MFDP was an open party in which no one was excluded because of their racial identity. This would have allowed African people in Mississippi to be able to participate in state politics. Fannie Lou Hamer was selected as the MFDP Congressional candidate.

In a move which was meant to retain southern support, President Lyndon Johnson decided to offer Hubert Humphrey the vice-presidency under the condition that he get the MFDP to back down. The pressure which the MFDP faced from the White House caused the coalition which the MFDP was working to build to dissolve as most of those who supported the MFDP withdrew. They did not want to oppose the Johnson-Humphrey team. The MFDP was being pressured into accepting a compromise in which the MFDP would receive two "at large" seats, while the entire Dixiecrat delegation were seated. The MFDP did not accept this compromise, since accepting such a compromise meant accepting a symbolic gesture. In the end, the MFDP had been rejected by the Democratic Party. Rather than supporting the MFDP, the Democratic Party sided with the state party in Mississippi which upheld racial segregation.

It became clear to Kwame Ture that African people could not rely on the Democratic Party. He went as far as comparing Africans joining the Democratic Party to Jews joining the Nazi party. SNCC was now leading the call for the creation of an independent party. This new political organization adopted a black panther as its symbol and became known as the Black Panther Party, though officially it was the Lowndes County Freedom Party. SNCC at this particular time was working on organizing an independent political party for African people in the United States. These attempts were ultimately unsuccessful, but I think the organizers in SNCC rightfully recognized that African people in the United States needed a political base which was independent of the Democratic Party. The problem was that many within the civil rights movement at the time were too attached to the Democratic Party to break with the Democrats. This is a point I made in *The Black African Crisis in the Age of a Black President.*

Lewis was one of those individuals who could not bring himself to oppose the Democratic establishment. Lewis was involved in what Malcolm X had termed the "Farce on Washington." During the famous 1963 march, Lewis was made to edit the speech which he originally planned to deliver because it was too critical of the Kennedy administration. Lewis demonstrated then that he could be controlled by those in power.

Lewis also demonstrated the limitations of attempting to reform an unjust and oppressive system from within. As a member of the House of Representatives, Lewis was in a position of real political power, but paradoxically Lewis had done more to effect change when he was an activist working for SNCC in the 1960s. Lewis sat in the Democratic Party, as the struggles against racial injustice were being waged by grassroots activists outside of the Democratic Party.

It became obvious that even with a black man as the president of America, African Americans still felt voiceless and frustrated, so they turned to mass demonstrations and public acts of protest to make their voices known. This frustration was not coming from the political establishment—it was not coming from individuals like Lewis and Obama. It was the ordinary citizens who were leading this charge. Colin Kaepernick, in particular, not only engaged in a very public act of protest against police brutality, but he also decided not to vote in 2016. He was criticized for this, but I understand it. A democracy offers citizens the freedom to vote, but Kaepernick was exercising his freedom not to vote because he did not believe that either political party was offering anything that he felt was worth voting for.

I mentioned the inability of the Democratic Party to defeat Donald Trump in 2016, which demonstrated how much the party had receded from the hope and optimism that managed to get Obama elected just eight years earlier. Trump was an extremely disliked presidential candidate, but so too was Hillary Clinton. In 2016 certain prominent members of the Democratic establishment— including First Lady Michelle Obama—resorted to cautioning Americans against voting for a third party because doing so could elect Trump. There was particular concern about the Green Party, which was blamed for helping George W. Bush win in 2000. I noted already that Kaepernick received criticism for his decision not to vote. I felt that rather than listening to those voices who were critical of the Democratic Party, Democrats and their supporters preferred to scare people into voting for Hillary Clinton by reinforcing the point that not doing so would get Trump elected. As it turns out, that strategy was not effective, and Trump was elected anyway. There were serious issues within the Democratic Party which I do not think the party was willing to address in 2016 and this is one of the reasons why they lost to Trump.

The Democratic Party has demonstrated that it is a seriously flawed party, but what can be done about this? Donald Trump obviously did not offer a better alternative and the Green Party had not established itself as a viable alternative, so one could rightfully conclude that the best strategy would be what Lewis did, which is to join the Democratic Party in order to reform the party. We found out in 2016 that the Democratic Party refused to be reformed, however, even if failure to reform meant risking losing the presidential election to Donald Trump.

Activists are always confronted with the choice of continuing to fight for change outside of the political system or joining the system to fight for change from the inside. As I noted already, Lewis was obviously one of those who decided to adopt the latter approach. What came out of the several decades that Lewis served as a congressman? He served from 1987 until his death in 2020. During that period of time Lewis had not managed to dramatically change the Democratic Party from the inside. He had not moved the party into a more progressive direction. I would argue that Lewis had more of a profound political impact on America as an organizer with SNCC than he did as a congressman.

I do understand the logic of wanting to get into politics to fight for change and to create reforms, but too often those who seek political positions become disconnected from the masses. This apparently happened when Marion Barry was elected as mayor. Charlie Cobb, who was a former staffer in SNCC, explained: "The guys in Anacostia don't really feel like they know Marion Barry anymore." So often it is the case that those who join the political system to create change end up being changed.

To Lewis' credit, I do not think he was one of those individuals who ever allowed his political position to change him very much, although this was perhaps because Lewis was always a very moderate figure. As I mentioned before, Lewis was the type of individual who could allow himself to be censored at the March on Washington. I wonder, how often during his time as a member of the Democratic Party had he censored himself by not speaking out against things that he disagreed with inside of the party?

In the end, I remember Lewis as a very brave and courageous man who risked his life for a noble cause. For this I honor him, although I cannot share certain aspects of his political views. Lewis once wrote: "I was beaten bloody by police officers. But I never hated them. I said, 'Thank you for your service.'" I am not one who advocates hate, but I also do not think that individuals should passively accept being beaten by police officers and then thank those police officers for engaging in such brutality. Behavior like this only emboldens oppressors to further engage in their acts of oppression, which is something that Kwame Ture understood more clearly than Lewis did. Indeed, there is a great deal to learn from both of these ancestors who were former chairpersons of SNCC.

2 RELIGION IN THE PAN-AFRICAN STRUGGLE

As a Pan-Africanist, the Abrahamic religions are of significance to me because, due to the global nature of these religions, they have had a very profound impact on the lives of African people, for better and for worse. I myself was raised in a Catholic environment. I went to a Catholic school. Both of my parents went to Catholic school and my mother remained a devout Catholic, so in my own life the influence of the Abrahamic religions played a significant role in my upbringing. This was at times a positive experience. I think the Catholic Church does offer some great values to live by, such as caring for others and striving to be a moral individual. But it is difficult to ignore that the Catholic Church also has a history of abuse, exploitation and violence. The Catholic Church is also a historically Eurocentric institution which has been guilty of whitewashing history, such as depicting Jesus as being white.

I think humans are instinctively drawn to the notion that we are more than just our physical selves and that there is more to our existence than the physical world. Religions are born out of this feeling of a deeper spiritual connection. Religions are rooted in the desire for self-improvement, the desire to be accepted and loved, and the desire to feel connected to other individuals. Religion also appeals to our desire to understand and explain the world around us, so religion appeals to very fundamental human yearnings.

It is true that many horrible actions have been committed in the name of religions, but I also think that religion can be a very powerful tool for transformation. Religions provide belief systems that can motivate people to do great things and to improve themselves. The best example of this that I have covered in my own writings is Malcolm X's transformation after becoming a Muslim, but there are certainly other examples that one can point to of religion transforming individuals in a positive manner. For some, religion was used as a rallying cry for rebellion in the struggle against oppression. For this reason, I do not think that religion is necessarily bad or inherently evil as some may argue.

One must first understand that religions at their core are merely ideas and concepts, and to the extent that one chooses to believe in these ideas one must use these ideas to serve one's interests. Jesus says in the Bible in Mark 2:27 that the Sabbath was made for man, not the man for Sabbath. I would argue that religions are made to serve the interests of people, rather than the other way around. It is for this reason that religion is not static and has constantly changed throughout history. This is not to suggest that the existence or non-existence of God rests on the validity of a particular religion. What I am suggesting is that religions are the product of human thought and human activity. The Bible and Qur'an were written by humans to be read by other humans. Religious doctrines and religious activity are not the product of God. These thoughts and actions are the product of human beings seeking to conceptualize and to understand God.

I stated before that the Abrahamic religions are of particular interest to me as a Pan-Africanist because these religions have had a very profound impact on African people. The role of Christianity and Islam in African history are especially controversial given how both religions are connected to the legacy of European and Arab imperialism in Africa. It was "God-fearing" Europeans and Arabs who enslaved, brutalized, tortured, raped and oppressed African people. For this reason, it is very difficult for some of us to separate these two religions from the history of our oppression. Some may hold the view that we should not separate these religions from that history at all, especially considering what the Bible and the Qur'an have to say about slavery.

The Christian Bible preaches that slaves should obey their masters at Ephesians 6:5. Leviticus 25:39-46 commands that Israelites are not to be made to work as slaves, but that the people from other nations may be bought as slaves and can be bequeathed to children as inherited property. Such enslaved individuals can also be made slaves for life. Chapter 33:50 of the Qur'an refers to captive (slave) women who are given to the Prophet Muhammad as spoils of war. The Qur'an does not condemn slavery, although chapter 24:33 of the Qur'an does encourage masters to allow their slaves to purchase their freedom. Critics of both religions rightfully note that neither holy book condemns slavery and that both books were used to justify the enslavement of African people.

Given the facts that I have presented, why then would any person of African descent practice religions whose holy books were used in our oppression and enslavement? Some would argue that we should not, but still many of us do practice these religions. A reason for this is that these religions were the religions of our conquerors and enslavers which were imposed on us through conquest. This is not a complete picture, however. The relationship between African people and these religions is a complex one and should not be reduced to merely pointing out the role that these religions played in our oppression.

In her autobiography, Assata Shakur mentions an exchange which she had with Kamau, who would become the father of her child. Kamau was a devout Muslim and was trying to get Assata to convert to Islam. Assata acknowledged the influence that Muslims had on the African American struggle due to figures such as Malcolm X and Elijah Muhammad, but she struggled with accepting belief in a loving and all-powerful being whose master plan included the enslavement of African people. I mention this exchange because it demonstrates the conflicting relationship that African people have had with religion. Some of us have viewed it as a tool of the oppressor which was imposed on us to rob us of our culture and maintain our oppression. For others, however, religion was used as a tool for struggle and for liberation. I would argue that both positions are valid, although they do conflict with each other.

Christianity and Islam emerged outside of Africa and outside of African culture, yet these religions do have their roots in Africa, specifically in Egyptian religious philosophy. This is a point that I made in *Malcolm X, Bob Marley, and Other Essays*. I mention this because one of Africa's great contributions to human civilization has been Africa's contributions to religion. I know some skeptics would balk at the notion that Africa's influence on the creation of the Abrahamic religions should be regarded as a contribution to human civilization, but, as I will explain, those religions were progressive within the context of the time and location in which those religions arose. I pointed out in *I Like What I Write* that Thomas Sankara viewed Jesus and Muhammad not as religious figures, but as revolutionaries who transformed the societies in which they lived. Regardless of what one thinks of Christianity and Islam, there is no denying the fact that both religions have certainly had a transformative impact on the societies in which these religions developed.

We can start with the religion of Christianity, which developed from the teachings of Jesus Christ. Jesus was someone who preached equality and peace. One of the most famous examples of this was when Jesus chased the money changers from out of a temple. This account is included in all four gospels. On another occasion, Jesus saved a woman who was about to be stoned to death for committing adultery. Jesus told the men who were about to stone her that the one without sin should be the one to throw the first stone. The message was clearly that we are all sinners and therefore we should not be so quick to condemn (or kill) others for their sins. Jesus chastised the wealthy elites, while affirming the humanity of the poor, the sinners, and others who were neglected or ridiculed in the society of Jesus' day.

One of the common criticisms of Christianity is that Jesus' idealistic pacifism is not a practical approach for confronting oppression. In Matthew 5, Jesus urges love for one's enemy and teaches that if a person is slapped in the face, that person should turn the other cheek to be slapped again. This passage is meant to promote brotherhood and peace, yet this is also a heavily criticized passage in the New Testament because it can be read as encouraging oppressed individuals to love the oppressor and passively accept oppression. Later in Matthew 26, Jesus rebukes one of his disciples for trying to defend him with a sword. In this chapter,

Jesus also utters one of the most famous phrases from the Bible, which is that those who take the sword shall die by the sword. The message clearly indicates that those who live a life of violence shall also die by violence. The irony of this is that Jesus was a man of non-violence and peace, yet he was killed in a very violent manner, so the impression given in the gospel of Matthew is that it is better to die violently than to use violence to protect yourself from those who wish to kill you.

The topic of non-violence was certainly one of the points of contention between the non-violent civil rights leaders like Martin Luther King and those in the Nation of Islam who rejected the "turn the other cheek" approach in favor of "an eye for an eye" approach to religion. The difference between the Nation of Islam and civil rights leaders on the question of violence was very apparent when Malcolm X shared a platform with Martin Luther King's brother, A.D. King. King, who shared his older brother's philosophy, told the audience that it is harder to hit a man who is praying and rendering the love of God. Malcolm's view on the topic of violence was that black people should not be fooled by "Uncle Tom Negro preachers" into not defending themselves.

Malcolm had also noted that black people had no problem engaging in violence when they were drafted by the United States in order to do so. He stated: "As long as the white man sent you to Korea, you bled. He sent you to Germany, you bled. He sent you to the South Pacific to fight the Japanese, you bled. You bleed for white people, but when it comes to seeing your own churches being bombed and little black girls murdered, you haven't got any blood. You bleed when the white man says bleed; you bite when the white man says bite; and you bark when the white man says bark."

The reality is that the extent to which Jesus preached passivity in the face of oppression is merely a matter of Biblical interpretation. As Malcolm X explained: "Jesus himself was ready to turn the synagogue inside out and upside down when things weren't going right. In fact, in the Book of Revelations, they've got Jesus sitting on a horse with a sword in his hand, getting ready to go into action." Martin Delany, Sam Sharpe, Julien Fedon, Harriet Tubman, and Nat Turner were examples of Christians who, like Jesus, were ready to go into action to liberate their people from the chains of slavery. It is also important to note that Mahatma Gandhi's non-violent struggle in India also influenced the non-violent philosophy of the civil rights movement, so the non-violent approach of the civil rights movement was not solely influenced by the teachings of Christ.

The Prophet Muhammad was also a transformative figure as well, although he was not a pacifist like Jesus was. Unlike Jesus, Muhammad was a skilled military commander who led several successful conquests. Whereas Christians view Jesus as being both the son of God and God incarnated as a man who was sent to die so that the sins of humanity may be forgiven, Muslims believe that Muhammad was chosen to be the last prophet of God (Qur'an 33:40) and that it was his mission to restore humankind to its proper state, which is submission to God. This also meant restoring a proper understanding of God. The Muslim understanding of God is not only one which differs from the Christian view of God, but it is one which is at times very critical of the Christian view.

Christians developed a doctrine known as the trinity, which views God in three distinct forms. In the Christian view God is the Father, the Son (Jesus), and the Holy Spirit. The Qur'an at chapter 4:171 specifically rejects the doctrine of the Trinity. Christianity also preached that Jesus is the way to salvation. Jesus himself proclaimed that he was the truth, the way, and the life, and that no one comes to the Father but through Jesus (John 14:6). Muslims view Jesus as one of the most important of God's prophets, but reject that Jesus was God incarnated in the flesh. The Qur'an also rejects the doctrine that Jesus was killed and resurrected, which is a central aspect of Christianity as well. Chapter 4:157-158 of the Qur'an suggests that Jesus was not killed at all. Chapter 9:29–33 offers a very sharp criticism of Jews who claim that Ezra is the son of Allah and Christians who claim that the Messiah is the son of Allah. This passage also claims that Muhammad was sent by Allah to manifest the religion of truth over all other religions. The relationship that Muslims have with Jews and Christians in the Qur'an is not always a contentious one, however. The Qur'an is very critical of Jews and Christians for their beliefs, yet Jews and Christians are also described as being "people of the book" in the Qur'an and are accorded with a level of respect which is not given to disbelievers. Chapter 2:62 proclaims that Jews and Christians who believe in Allah and do righteous deeds shall be rewarded.

Muhammad was persecuted by the people of Mecca because of his teachings. Muhammad went to war with Mecca and eventually prevailed. Through military conquests Muhammad was able to gain control of most of Arabia. As I mentioned before, Muhammad certainly was no pacifist. When he and his followers were threatened, they did not hesitate to pick up the sword to defend themselves and to eventually seize power. With that power Muhammad implemented reforms, such as calling for an end to infanticide (17:31). Muhammad also outlawed compulsion in religion (2:256) and called on wealth to be given to the needy (2:177). Muhammad did not outlaw slavery, but he did encourage masters to free those slaves who desired to be free.

Whereas the gospels tell the story of Jesus' life, the Qur'an contains very little biographical information about Muhammad. The Qur'an is not a narrative of Muhammad's life and the Qur'an offers very little insight into Muhammad's personal life. This seems to be because the Qur'an was more concerned about what Muhammad preached than with who Muhammad was.

One important difference between Islam and previous religions is that Muslims do not follow a particular individual. As Malcolm X explained in one of his speeches which was delivered when he was a minister with the Nation of Islam, Judaism is named after Judah, Christianity is named after Jesus Christ, and Buddhism is named after Buddha. These three religions, as Malcolm pointed out, were named after individual men, whereas Islam means submission to God. Chronologically speaking Islam came after Judaism and Christianity, but the point that Malcolm was making is that the prophets in the Bible served God. They did not practice a defined religion called Judaism or Christianity; they merely submitted to God. This was one way in which Islam distinguished itself from some of the religions which came before. Malcolm was not practicing orthodox Islam at the time, but the argument that he made regarding Islam being the true religion of God is one that many orthodox Muslims make. They claim that to be a Muslim is to be in a state of submission to God and that the first man to submit to God was Adam, therefore making Adam the first Muslim. For this reason, Muslims hold the view that Islam has existed for as long as humans have existed.

I briefly gave this description of Christianity and Islam so one can understand that these religions were religions which did have a transformative impact on the societies in which they emerged. With that being established, both religions were also used as tools in the oppression and enslavement of African people as well. In response to this oppression there have been religious sects which have tried to Africanize the Abrahamic religions to help empower African people. The two which I shall deal with specifically are Rastafarians and the Nation of Islam, which are two religious movements which have left a very profound mark on the struggles of African people. Both movements have certainly influenced my own development and understanding of the Pan-African struggle.

Rastas developed a religious belief system rooted in Christianity, but this religious belief system was also heavily influenced by the teachings of Marcus Garvey. Rastas believe that the Ethiopian emperor Haile Selassie was God incarnated as a man, hence why they are called Rastafarians; named after Ras Tafari, which was Selassie's name before he was crowned as emperor. Haile Selassie was a Christian who never purported to be a divine figure. Selassie was actually a very deeply flawed emperor and the legacy that he left behind in Ethiopia was at best a very complicated one, but to Rastas, Haile Selassie was God.

Rastas are also known for wearing dreadlocks. The early Rastas did not wear dreadlocks, but this practice was adopted around the 1940s and 1950s. The Jamaican scholar Horace Campbell held the view that Rastas began wearing dreadlocks after seeing photographs of the Mau Mau rebels in Kenya. Youth Black Faith was credited with being the Rasta group that popularized the wearing of dreadlocks. Youth Black Faith was an anti-colonial group which actively supported the liberation struggle in Kenya. The wearing of dreadlocks was also an act of defiance against the social norms of Jamaican society at the time.

My mother often "grounded" with Rastas in Guyana. She was not a Rasta herself, but they respected her, nonetheless. My mother especially came to enjoy Rastafarian food, which Rastas refer to as "ital." She also learned how to skank, which is a type of dance which is performed to reggae music. Rastas became a very important element in shaping post-colonial Caribbean society, especially due to the music of Bob Marley and other artists who used the reggae art form as a means to spread their ideas.

Much like Rastas, the Nation of Islam developed a uniquely *black* version of an Abrahamic religion, although the Nation of Islam's brand of Islam departs greatly from orthodox Islam. One significant difference is that the Nation of Islam believes that Wallace Fard Muhammad was God and that Fard had taught Elijah Poole—later Elijah Muhammad—the true history of the black man. This history departs greatly from what the Qur'an teaches about Islam.

Fard founded the Nation of Islam in the 1930s. As Fard began preaching, his following grew and at Fard's meetings no white people were allowed to enter. Fard was described as a tireless teacher, who worked without sleep. According to one story, Elijah Muhammad peeped into the keyhole of Fard's hotel room door to see if Fard was sleeping. Elijah Muhammad looked inside and saw Fard standing in front of a mirror, looking into the mirror at the keyhole behind him.

Not very much is known about Fard. Fard told Elijah Muhammad that he came from Mecca, but precisely when and where Fard was born appears to be a mystery. His racial identity has also been contested, with some suggesting that he was of Turkish or Persian ancestry, while other accounts suggest that Fard was a black man who was born to a Syrian father. Fard's disappearance is also a mystery. Fard disappeared in 1934, leaving Elijah Muhammad in charge of the Nation of Islam. Some maintained that Fard returned to Mecca. Elijah Muhammad explained that Fard moved to Chicago and then continued to travel throughout America. After Fard disappeared, Elijah Muhammad began preaching that Fard was God. This sense of mystery surrounding Fard helped to reinforce the notion of his divine nature.

According to the doctrine of the Nation of Islam, white people are a race of devils who were created by a scientist named Yakub. The rule of the devil race was to last 6,000 years. These teachings are nowhere to be found in the Bible or the Qur'an. The teaching of the Nation of Islam was obviously one that was very race-centered because it was aimed specifically at African Americans who were being oppressed in a racist society. Another major difference is that, unlike orthodox Muslims, members of the Nation of Islam do not believe in an afterlife. According to Fard's teachings, heaven and hell were not locations that one goes to after dying but were states of minds. For this reason, ministers in the Nation of Islam spoke of raising the dead as raising the unconsciousness of those who were mentally dead, rather than a physical resurrection.

The religion of Islam rejects the view that Jesus

was crucified and rose from the dead. The Qur'an chapter 4:157 clearly declares that Jesus was not killed or crucified. The Nation of Islam holds the same view. Revelation 1:5 refers to Jesus as the first begotten of the dead, but as the Nation of Islam has pointed out, Jesus actually was not the first person to rise from the dead in the Bible. One of the miracles that Jesus was said to have performed was raising Lazarus from the dead. In the Old Testament, Elijah also called on God to bring back to life the child of a widow after the child died due to an illness. For this reason, the Nation of Islam viewed the reference to the begotten of the dead to be a reference to the mentally dead.

The Nation of Islam also parted with the philosophy of turning the other cheek and praying for the enemy. Instead, the Nation of Islam prayed for God's wrath to be inflicted upon the white race. This was something that Malcolm himself did often. Malcolm described a plane crash in France which killed white Americans as being an act of God. On another occasion, Malcolm stated, "I pray that God will strike 'em [...] put death in their family [...] I pray that God will bring that on." When Phil Graham committed suicide, Malcolm joked that "in a moment of happiness" Graham had blown his own brains out. Malcolm added, "I love to see them get that happy." The God which the Nation of Islam prayed to was one which sought to avenge the suffering of black people.

Any religion which teaches the oppressed to love and pray for their oppressor is a religion which is teaching the oppressed to accept their plight and to not resist. This is the type of religion preached by a slave master. I mentioned before that the Bible teaches that slaves should obey their masters. Jesus himself told his followers to love thy enemy and pray for those who persecute you. The Bible is the same book which also tells of God delivering the Hebrew people out of slavery in Egypt and drowning the pharaoh who was trying to recapture them. For this reason, one's interpretation of the Bible is important in determining how one views the Bible. I know Christians believe that the Bible is the word of God and that we need to follow everything that Jesus teaches in the Bible, but Harriet Tubman was no less of a Christian for praying for the death of her slave master. Nat Turner was no less of a Christian for killing slave masters rather than loving them. Thomas Sankara made it very clear that the Bible and Qur'an cannot serve the oppressed and the oppressor in the same way. This means that to the extent that a religious text preaches passivity in the face of oppression, then that religious text must be contradicted if doing so furthers the cause of justice and liberation from oppression.

The fact that established religious institutions helped to uphold the institution of slavery meant that Africans had to break with some of those religious institutions in their struggle for liberation. Often Africans who broke with those institutions did not completely reject religion, but were instead rejecting the interpretation of the slave master. I quote Marcus J. de Carvalho, who wrote in *The*

Human Tradition in Modern Brazil about Agostinho José Pereira: "In Brazil the rigidity of the Catholic hierarchy and the cooperation between Church and state made it difficult for a black man to become a priest. Besides, it would have been difficult for any Catholic priest to preach a message of rebellion to slaves without breaking with the Church hierarchy and thereby with Catholicism itself. Agostinho broke with the Church by attributing his ministry to a divine revelation unmediated by priestly authority." Carvalho also questioned whether or not Agostinho understood the political implications of his ministry. Agostinho claimed that he was a follower of "the law of Jesus Christ" and may well have viewed himself as a preacher. Whatever the case may have been, the fact is clear that Agostinho was a preacher who defied the established religious order of his day.

Karl Marx very famously described religion as the opium of the masses. This is not a generalization that I think can be maintained in light of the various examples of religious individuals who have been motivated to struggle, but I do recognize that in many cases religion causes individuals to become meek and docile in the face of injustice and oppression. Religion is very political, but some are so enamored with the sanctity of religious tradition and are so focused on seeking rewards in the hereafter that they do not recognize the political nature of religion.

Recognizing the political nature of religion is important because it means recognizing that religions are just as much political as they are spiritual. I repeat again that religions are created by humans to serve the interest of humans. The Bible, for example, was written by individuals who lived in a society where slavery was an accepted practice and for this reason slavery is never viewed as being a sin in the Bible. This is why I make the point that Christianity and Islam were progressive relative to the societies from which they emerged, but both religions were also a product of the societies from which they emerged from. This meant that the political realities of the day undoubtedly influenced these religions and therefore one cannot separate religion from the politics of the society from which those religions emerged.

The Old Testament is the story of the Hebrews; a people who were rescued from being enslaved in Egypt. The Hebrews went on to wage wars against the Canaanites and other groups in the area. The Hebrews eventually prevailed and established the Kingdom of Israel. This united kingdom then split into two smaller kingdoms; the Kingdom of Israel and the Kingdom of Judah. The Old Testament is not merely the story of an all-powerful supreme being who created the earth. The Old Testament is a story of a people rising out of slavery and building a kingdom. The Old Testament is a political story which depicts the Hebrews engaging in political actions, such as fighting wars and building kingdoms. One can debate the historicity of the Bible's accounts of the Hebrew people, but that is not my point here. My point is that the Old Testament of the Bible is also a political text. The

Hebrews did not patiently endure slavery, hoping for a reward in the hereafter.

We also see the influence of politics when examining the life and death of Jesus. Jesus stated in Matthew 22:21, render unto Caesar that which belongs to Caesar and render unto God that which belongs to God in response to a question about whether or not Jesus believed that it was lawful to pay taxes to the Roman Empire. This passage indicated that Jesus did not seek to undermine the political authority of the Roman Empire, but he was viewed as a threat nevertheless because of his religious teachings. John 19 explains that Jesus was condemned to be crucified not by the Roman governor Pontius Pilate, but by the Jews who believed that Jesus was a threat to the political status quo. Jesus was accused of opposing Caesar (John 19:12). Muhammad was a political figure as well. Apart from being a prophet, Muhammad was also a statesman who established political control over the territories which he conquered. This is why I maintain that religions are political as well.

Given the political nature of religion, they have often been utilized by conquerors and colonizers who seek to impose their domination over the oppressed. Others utilized the political elements of religion to oppose oppression and to fight for justice. The Nation of Islam was not a political organization per se, but one thing that I do admire the Nation of Islam for is that the organization did not shun taking political positions, such as opposing American militarism overseas. This is why the Nation of Islam opposed the Vietnam War. I agree that religion should not play a role in politics insofar as I do not believe that politicians should impose their own personal religious beliefs on the masses, but I also hold the view that religious people should not hesitate to take stands on political issues, such as the stand that Muhammad Ali and Martin Luther King took when they opposed the Vietnam War.

Malcolm's eventual split from the Nation of Islam and his embrace of orthodox Islam is a topic I have addressed in other written works, so I will not rehash that here. What I do intend to explain, however, is that despite the problems with the Nation of Islam's doctrine, the Nation of Islam did achieve a great deal which should not be dismissed or forgotten because of the negative aspects of the organization.

It is very difficult for some to reconcile the great works that the Nation of Islam has done with Malcolm's assassination, Elijah Muhammad's extramarital affairs, and other problems which arose within the organization. Elijah Muhammad's conduct, in particular, is a point of great criticism. After all, how can a religious leader preach morality and sexual discipline to his followers, yet have numerous affairs with much younger women, impregnating them and then punishing those women for immoral behavior?

The history of religion is filled with individuals who preached righteousness and practiced the opposite, so Elijah Muhammad is not unique in that regard. Elijah Muhammad's private conduct does raise the question of accountability, however. Within the Nation of Islam, Elijah Muhammad was viewed as God's messenger and to go against him would be to go against the very message of God. This is why some in the Nation of Islam viewed Malcolm's assassination as a form of divine punishment. This is where religion becomes dangerous. Followers of a particular religion can become so dogmatic and inflexible in their views that they respond violently to opposing views, even if such opposing views are presented peacefully or non-violently. At no point did Malcolm make violent threats against Elijah Muhammad, yet members of the Nation of Islam concluded that Malcolm deserved death for daring to voice his disagreements with the Nation of Islam.

With religious organizations there is always the concern about the development of personality cults. There was certainly an element of this within the Nation of Islam. Elijah Muhammad claimed that he was a messenger of God. As such, there was no one above Elijah Muhammad within the Nation of Islam and no one who was qualified to challenge Elijah Muhammad's authority. A more extreme example of a religious cult would be Jim Jones' People's Temple, which ended up killing hundreds of its own followers. The Nation of Islam certainly was never as extreme as the People's Temple, but those cultish tendencies did exist in the Nation of Islam, as Malcolm's split with the Nation of Islam demonstrated.

When an individual is able to convince his or her followers that the individual is a deity or was appointed by a deity, it does create a dangerous situation in which the followers believe that the individual which they are following is divine and infallible. This situation is ripe for abuse on the part of such religious leaders, yet I would also argue that this problem is not unique to religious organizations. The Black Panther Party was a secular organization that preached the materialist doctrine of Marxism-Leninism, yet the Black Panther Party developed cultish tendencies around the leadership of Huey Newton, which I discussed in some detail in *Africa-Man: A Collection of Pan-African Writings*. I mention this to make the point that even without belief in a divine and unseen force, personality cults can still emerge within organizations.

To properly address this issue there must be some sort of checks and balances to keep the leader accountable to the followers. In the Yoruba kingdom of Oyo, for example, the ruling king was viewed as being a semi-divine figure. Despite this, the ruler of Oyo was not held to be an infallible ruler who was divinely appointed to rule without challenge. For those who misruled or were incompetent there was a very severe punishment. Kings of Oyo who were found to have failed in their duty as king were made to commit a ritualistic act of suicide. In many African kingdoms, the king was seen as a religious figure. This obviously gave the ruling king power and authority beyond that of an ordinary person, but this also meant that the king had greater responsibilities than that of ordinary individuals as well.

The Rastas and the Nation of Islam are religious movements which do deserve credit for helping to uplift African people through raising our consciousness and pride in ourselves. What is also noteworthy is that both religious movements began among the poor and dispossessed masses, rather than among the more affluent segment of the African population, whose religious orientation was largely connected to Eurocentric Christianity. Despite the shortcomings of both religious movements, I think they are great examples of how African people should adopt religious philosophies in a manner which advances our liberation.

There is also the question of atheism. I want to focus particularly on Marxism, since Marxism not only presents an atheist worldview, but also offers its own vision of salvation from oppressive and exploitative forces. Marxism or communism adheres to a strictly materialist view of the world and views human progress as being rooted in labor and production. Marx was concerned about the material world and how people operate within the material world, as opposed to a spiritual realm which cannot be seen or understood by mortals. Marx was an atheist and many prominent Marxists shared Marx's atheism. Vladimir Lenin was an atheist who was very critical of religion and the Soviet Union was established as an atheist state. Not all Marxists have adopted atheism, however. Kwame Nkrumah explained: "I am a non-denominational Christian and a Marxist socialist and I have not found any contradiction between the two."

Contradictions between Marxism and Christianity do exist. The most obvious contradiction between Marxism and Christianity is that Marx was a materialist and an atheist, whereas Christianity concerns itself with the immaterial world and Christians obviously believe in God. With that being established, there are also certain similarities that one can point to as well. Much like Marx, Jesus was concerned with wealth inequality and the exploitation of the poor. The Bible contains the story of Jesus' encounter with a rich man who wanted to obtain eternal life. Jesus responded by telling the rich man to sell all of his possessions and to give his money to the poor. Jesus also informed this man that it is easier for a camel to pass through the eye of a needle than for a rich man to enter into heaven. Jesus' view of the rich is further illustrated in the gospel of Luke, which contains the story of a rich man and a beggar named Lazarus. When Lazarus died, he was taken by angels to be at Abraham's side. When the rich man died, he was taken to Hades where he was tormented. When the rich man begged Abraham to have pity on him, Abraham replied by reminding the rich man that he had received good things in life, while Lazarus received bad things. Here we see that in Jesus' teachings those who live in opulence have no place in heaven after they die.

Jesus and Marx held the same view that wealth inequality was a wrong which needed to be corrected. Of course, the solution which both men presented to this inequality differed. Marx believed that the working class had to rise up and overthrow the capitalist class, creating a new society. Jesus' approach was one rooted in the belief that rich people are excluded from heaven, unless they shed their worldly possessions and give their wealth to the poor. Marx, the materialist, was concerned with changing the material conditions of oppressed workers, whereas Jesus was more concerned with justice in the spiritual hereafter. The two traditions are certainly different, but I do not think that they were completely irreconcilable either.

Marxism developed in a very similar manner to how religions developed. Many world religions developed because a particular individual began preaching a doctrine which was meant to transform the societies in which that individual lived. These religious leaders promised eventual human salvation. Marx was not viewed as a religious leader, but he can be compared to a Biblical prophet in the sense that he foretold of an inevitable class conflict which will finally bring an end to capitalist exploitation. Marx did not promise salvation in the hereafter and his writings were grounded in material realities which can be observed as opposed to that which is merely felt or is believed, but Marxism brought forward a vision for the creation of a better society and this vision inspired hope.

Communism has also been subject to some of the same type of sectarian squabbles that have been common in religion. Communism became a global ideology due in large part to the successes of the revolution in Russia, which brought Vladimir Lenin into power. Mao Zedong would lead a communist revolution of his own in China. China and the Soviet Union became the two leading communist nations in the world. A dispute arose between the two nations over differing interpretations of communism. There were even conflicts over communism within the Soviet Union itself, as Joseph Stalin and Leon Trotsky struggled for power in the Soviet Union when Lenin died. This struggle resulted in Trotsky being exiled from the Soviet Union and assassinated.

In African religions there were no religious prophets such as Jesus, Muhammad, Jeremiah, Moses, Daniel, and others who preached the message of God in the Bible and the Qur'an. Some African religions have spirits which serve as guides. For example, the Yoruba people have the Orishas. These spirits often serve as intermediaries between the living world and the spiritual realm, but the spirits do not set out to convert people or to spread a particular religious message.

Proselytizing is also not a typical aspect of African religions. The tolerance of opposing religious ideas was one of the reasons why foreign religions were able to take root in Africa and spread. Christians were persecuted in Rome, but they found refuge in Africa. Likewise, Muhammad and his followers were persecuted in Arabia, but found refuge in Africa. I do not think that religions necessarily have to be in conflict with each other. When asked if he denied that there is a Christian God, Malcolm X explained that Muslims believe in the God that created the universe, which is the same God that Christians and Jews believe in. Indeed, several religions do speak of a singular God who created the universe, although the name used for that being varies across religions and cultures. African societies were societies which traditionally did not seek to impose their religious ideas or their concepts of God unto other people.

Yet another criticism of religion is that religion hinders scientific progress. Certainly, the Christian Church at a particular point in Europe's history was hostile to science because science was viewed as a threat to the established religious order. One of the points that I made in *The Black African Crisis in the Age of a Black President* was that Western civilization has typically been hostile towards new ideas which threaten the religious status quo. I specifically mention the examples of Socrates who was made to drink poison after he was found guilty of not believing in the gods of Athens and Giordano Bruno who was burned at the stake for holding scientific views which differed with the Catholic Church. This was not the case in African societies, however.

It is true that African religions were often deeply steeped in superstition rooted in a limited scientific understanding of the world, but this does not mean that African societies rejected scientific inquiry. In some cases, there was even a direct connection between African religious beliefs and scientific inquiry. Shango became the lightning deity among the Yoruba people because Shango was known for conducting experiments to attract lightning. He was too successful at this and one day lightning struck his palace, burning it down. This was long before Benjamin Franklin's kite experiment.

Colonial narratives of African people have tended to depict us as ignorant and primitive savages, who engaged in superstitious rituals or devilish voodoo sacrifices. The missionary work which Christians engaged in was meant to save African people from these heathen rituals. In some cases, the missionary work in Africa did leave a positive mark by putting an end to some of the more backwards traditional practices (such as killing twins, which was done in some parts of Africa), but this missionary work also often failed to respect the traditions that African people had in place. Traditions and beliefs which were seen as primitive or superstitious often had a very rational or practical basis, such as preserving and protecting the environment out of the belief that nature possesses a spirit which must be respected.

The foreign Christians and Muslims who came into Africa had little respect for Africa's traditional religions and sadly many Africans who have adopted these foreign religious ideologies have a similar disregard and scorn for Africa's traditional religious philosophy, despite the fact that African religious traditions influenced the creation of the Abrahamic religions. Even so, there is no denying that the Abrahamic religions have also played an important role in the struggles of African people. This is not to suggest that the influence of the Abrahamic religions have been wholly positive, but the influence was not wholly negative either.

45

3 FROM OPPOSITION TO COALITION: LESSONS FROM THE WPA

In 2015, a political coalition which consisted of A Partnership for National Unity (APNU) and the Alliance for Change (AFC) won the elections in Guyana. This coalition of political forces managed to unseat the incumbent People's Progressive Party (PPP), which had been in power in Guyana since 1992. This was a very welcomed development in Guyana. During the time that the PPP had been in power, it engaged in behavior which, as Guyanese political activist Eusi Kwayana stated, made the PPP "objectionable to man and God." Ralph Ramkarran, who served as a minister in the PPP, eventually resigned over the corruption. Ramkarran publicly criticized the corruption within the PPP and he was denounced by the PPP for doing this. The expectation was that members of the PPP were to remain silent over the blatant corruption.

The victory in 2015 was hardly surprising to me since the PPP failed to win a majority of the votes in 2011. I quote Kwayana again, who stated that the election in 2011 "was nobody's victory." The PPP took control of the government, but the opposition had control of the parliament. President Donald Ramotar claimed that the opposition had rigged the election, which was his way of trying to explain the PPP's disappointing electoral results. The reality is that the PPP had made the mistake of relying too strongly on racial politics. In the state owned newspaper, the *Chronicle*, the government stated that it owed its electoral success to the Indian majority in Guyana, which helped to entrench the feeling of racial domination in Guyana. On another occasion, activists in Guyana staged a protest of the *Chronicle* by burning editions of the newspaper in response to an editorial which was published which stated that African Guyanese were being groomed to attack and kill Indians in Guyana.

One incident which truly demonstrates the cruel nature of the PPP government were the protests which took place in Linden in response to the government's decision to increase electricity rates in Linden. The residents of Linden complained that they could not afford the increase, and that Linden needed jobs, not a tax increase. One resident complained that President Ramotar promised 2,000 new jobs in Linden, but the promise never materialized. Some in Linden felt that the increase in electricity rates was to punish the people of Linden for overwhelmingly voting in favor of the opposition. Despite the fact that the unemployment rate in Linden was at 70%, Prime Minister Sam Hinds defended the government's decision to increase taxes on Linden.

The protests turned into a tragedy. The police opened fire on the protesters, killing three men and wounding several more. This did not quell the protests, however. Residents began burning tires and debris to create a blockade. This incident demonstrated the lack of regard with which the PPP treated poor and struggling Guyanese citizens.

There was a sense that in 2011 a government of national unity should have been established, since no particular political party won that election. Kwayana described the electoral results as a "moment for healing" in Guyana since the Guyanese people voted in such a way that there was no outright winner in the election. The political leaders did not see it this way, however. The PPP took control of the presidency but remained a minority within the National Assembly. In 2011, the APNU and AFC had not yet formed a political coalition, but they were the two largest opposition parties in Guyana. The two parties joined together in 2015 and subsequently contested the election that year.

Of particular interest to me was the fact that the WPA and the PNC were now in the same government. Both the PNC and the WPA were members of the APNU coalition. Prior to 1992, the PNC had been in power in Guyana and the WPA was one of the leading opposition parties against the PNC. The WPA, as the name suggests, was a political party which was organized to advance the interests of working class Guyanese. The WPA was especially critical of the corruption and abuse of power which occurred under the government of Forbes Burnham, who was the prime minister (later president) of Guyana at the time.

During the 1970s, Walter Rodney stood out as the most notable personality within the WPA. He was especially critical of the misrule of Burnham and how that misrule adversely impacted the lives of the working people in Guyana. One element of this misrule which Rodney discussed in a film titled *In the Sky's Wild Noise* was the manner in which the government of Guyana had become the largest employer in the nation due to the fact that it had nationalised several industries. Rodney explained that "it is unnecessary to threaten a man's life and liberty if by the fundamental threat to his capacity to earn and survive you can reduce him to a state of submission, and this is continually what is taking place."

The point which Rodney was making is that the government in Guyana maintained control over the means of production, which allowed the government to exercise very strong political control over the masses without necessarily having to resort to force and violence. This is not to say that the government did not resort to these things, however. As I pointed out in my book, *The Intellectual and Political Legacy of Walter Rodney*, the PNC government did in fact resort to violence against critics of the government. Rodney himself was a victim of this. He was assassinated at the hands of the government.

Given this history, I was interested to see that the

WPA (Rodney's party) and the PNC (Burnham's party) were now in the government together. I was especially interested to see what role the WPA would play within this new government. The PNC, being the largest party in the coalition, took a leadership role. When the APNU+AFC coalition won, it was David Granger of the PNC who became the president of the country. Moses Nagamootoo of the AFC became the prime minister. Not only was the APNU+AFC facing the task of holding together this coalition as it was attempting to manage the country, but the APNU+AFC retained a single seat majority in the National Assembly.

The newly elected government engaged in the very opportunism which the WPA had opposed during Burnham's time. The new government wasted little time in increasing the salary of government ministers by 50%. How could a government justify increasing its salary in a country like Guyana with so many poor and struggling individuals? Joseph Harmon, the Minister of State, declared that he would offer no apology for the pay increase in response to the criticism which the government was receiving. He actually defended the pay increase by arguing that ministers deserved to be paid more and that under the previous administration ministers accepted a smaller salary because they were engaged in corrupt practices.

It was also revealed that the government was paying $500,000 a month in rent for ministers Simona Broomes and Valerie Adams-Patterson. David Hinds, an executive member of the WPA, denounced this as being immoral, considering the financial struggles of the rest of the population. Hinds pointed out that it was a struggle to get salary increases for public servants and teachers, while the government had no problem spending large sums of money to house government ministers. Hinds also argued that a proposed $300,000 limit for house rent was still too high. The WPA's position was that the ministers should pay their own rent or be housed in government properties. Just as he defended the salary increase, Harmon also defended the $500,000 house rent by stating that this was part of the benefit which was given to ministers.

Both members and supporters of the WPA complained about the WPA's relationship with the government, as well as the WPA's relative silence on perceived missteps by the government. When the government won, the WPA was not consulted. No meeting was held between the WPA and President Granger to discuss the role that the WPA would have in the government. It was very clear that the WPA was not being respected inside of the coalition.

Hinds was eventually terminated from the *Chronicle*, along with Lincoln Lewis who, like Hinds, was critical of the government's performance. Three board members resigned in protest. Journalist Ruel Johnson also resigned as well. When questioned about this, President Granger explained that he does not run the *Chronicle* and that he did not inquire into the situation to find out why Lewis and Hinds were released. Granger also added that "an editor does what an editor does."

The WPA was in a similar situation to the one that the National Joint Action Committee (NJAC) in Trinidad was in. Like the WPA, NJAC was founded during the Black Power movement which was sweeping throughout the Caribbean region. Makandal Daaga, NJAC's chief servant, played a leading role in the 1970 Black Power uprising, which I wrote about in *Malcolm X, Bob Marley, and Other Essays*. NJAC joined the People's Partnership coalition, which was elected to power in 2010. That coalition was led by the United National Congress (UNC). As I have written elsewhere, this was viewed as a betrayal of the principles which Daaga and NJAC fought for in the 1970s. The APNU+AFC coalition in Guyana only lasted one term, just as the People's Partnership coalition in Trinidad did.

The WPA and NJAC were established political parties which were known for their staunch opposition and resistance as opposition parties, but neither party was ever able to amass a large enough following to win an election. Part of this is because of the racially divided nature of Trinidadian and Guyanese politics. In Guyana the PNC is perceived as being an African party and the PNM is viewed as an African party in Trinidad, whereas the PPP and UNC are perceived to be Indian parties. I use the word perceived because the reality is that the major political parties in Guyana and Trinidad do not truly represent the interests of the working class. This is why the PNC government could so comfortably raise its salary in a country where so many of the African citizens are struggling to survive.

Although politics in Trinidad is often perceived along racial lines, Chalkdust pointed out in "Too Much Party" that these parties have very little to do with race or religion. He sings:

This thing called PNM
This thing called UNC
Is only a power play to get our sympathy
Is not 'bout African
It's neither East Indian
It ain't have nothing to do with anybody's religion
Kamaluddin is a Muslim
Mahabir, Christian to the brim
Yet Montano the mulatto
Different race same party you know
Ronnie Williams and Max Awon
Are two Chinese politicians
And while both of them love PNM
Brian Kuei Tung had a problem

The point that Chalkdust was making is that political parties have little to do with race and that political leaders themselves are frequently switching from one party to another party. He intones: "Rich men does be supporting who they think going to win/Loyalty, friends, means nothing, money is their thing." Chalkdust gives examples of Kuei Tung and Hector McClean who both switched from PNM to UNC, and Augustus Ramrekersingh who was a member of Tapia and became a minister with the PNM.

I mention Chalkdust here because as an artist he has used his music to criticize the nature of politics in Trinidad. Whereas Daaga was drawn into electoral politics in Trinidad and became a member of the coalition government there, Chalkdust remained outside of the political structure and remained a voice for the masses in Trinidad. This is significant to note here because during the Black Power movement in Trinidad in the 1970s, it was political activists such as Daaga and calypsonians such as Chalkdust who offered the most scathing criticisms of the state of the country under the leadership of Eric Williams. The difference between the two men, as noted before, is that Daaga was eventually drawn into electoral politics, whereas Chalkdust remained outside of the political system, while continuing his critique of those who are in power. In "The Tent Is It," Chalkdust proclaims that his political allegiance is to poor people:

I am for PPP
The Poor People's Party
Is them I represent
And the kaiso tent
Is my parliament

Chalkdust's criticism of political parties in Trinidad can be contrasted with the Mighty Gabby from Barbados. The Mighty Gabby used his music to denounce some of the policies of Prime Minister Tom Adams of the Barbados Labour Party. "Boots," which criticized the government for spending taxpayers' money on equipping soldiers in a country with high rates of unemployment and a depleted treasury, was banned in Barbados. Gabby, whose real name is Anthony Carter, would appear in the 1994 manifesto of the Democratic Labour Party as one of the political candidates of the DLP. Gabby would soon switch political allegiances and became a supporter of the BLP. Gabby responded to those who criticized him for switching his political alliances in "Gabby is Bee," in which he sang:

All a dem calypsonian cussin' me
Because I hook up with the BLP
When I was supporting the Dems
All a dem claim dem was my friends
I exercise my democracy
Now they want to kill me

In the song Gabby specifically attacked Romeo, Kid Site and Classic for criticizing him over his decision to support the BLP. Gabby was certainly exercising his democratic right to align himself with whichever party he wanted to, but this was coming from the same calypsonian who had previously explained in "Wind Force" that his philosophy is that the country must come before party, and that the DLP and BLP share the same philosophy.

Within politics in post-colonial societies it is not uncommon to find cases where individuals who opposed a particular government or political party find themselves being drawn into that party. One can look to Togo as an example. In 2010, Gilchrist Olympio, the leader of the main opposition party, the Union des Forces de Changement (UFC), and the son of Togo's first president Sylvanus Olympio, opted to form a unity government with the ruling political party, the Rassemblement du Peuple Togolais (RPT). The RPT was the political party which was created by Gnassingbé Eyadéma. Eyadéma came to power through a military coup in 1967 and remained in power until his death in 2005. After that his son Faure Gnassingbé was installed by the military. Not only was Gilchrist Olympio's decision to join with the government seen as a betrayal in the eyes of many of the Togolese people, but Gilchrist Olympio was joining with the very forces which assassinated his father.

Togo is a rather extreme example given the brutal nature of the military regime there. Certainly, Guyana, Trinidad, and Barbados have never experienced that level of political repression, but Togo is mentioned to provide yet another example of how opposition leaders allow themselves to be co-opted by those in positions of political power. This is done because those in the opposition are not seeking to truly transform the society. Those in political opposition often seek to replace the political leaders in order to reap the benefits of the exploitative system and when having failed to do so, those opposition figures will cease being in the opposition and seek alliances with the party in power for opportunistic reasons.

To return to the WPA in Guyana, in the past the WPA had formed a coalition with the PPP for the purpose of removing the incumbent PNC. In 2015 the situation had changed and the WPA was now part of the coalition which removed the PPP. This marked the first time that the WPA was a member of an incumbent government, although it was very apparent that the WPA did not occupy a significant role within this new government and that this new government was engaged in policies which were contrary to the values which the WPA espoused. Despite this, the WPA opted to remain in the government, with nothing to show for it. The APNU+AFC coalition would be defeated by the PPP in 2020, lasting only one term in power just like the PP coalition in Trinidad.

The logic of entering into the system to create change from the inside is that change is a gradual, but certain process and that it would be better to make compromises by working inside of a corrupt political system than continuously opposing the system from the outside. As we saw with the WPA, this tactic was not particularly effective in the short-term nor the long-term.

4 PAN-AFRICANISM IN POST-COLONIAL SOCIETIES: WALTER RODNEY AND THE CRISIS OF THE PERIPHERY

In a lecture titled "Crisis in the Periphery: Africa and the Caribbean," Walter Rodney spoke at length about some of the challenges which confronted post-colonial societies in Africa and the Caribbean. Not only did he speak about the reactionary leadership which took power and maintained the prior colonial system, but he also spoke about the challenge of developing a proper ideological approach to addressing this crisis in post-colonial societies.

African and Caribbean societies were emerging into independence out of the trauma and the hardships of the colonial period. This period also witnessed the emergence of a particular type of leadership which perpetuated the brutality and the viciousness of the prior colonial system.

In *Colonialism and Violence in Nigeria*, Toyin Falola notes that various Igbo groups engaged in wars with the British between 1901 and 1917. I specifically reference the Igbo resistance since the Igbo people were organized in village governments rather than under a more centralized form of governance, as was the case for other ethnic groups in Nigeria, such as the Yoruba and the Hausa. One British officer who was involved in the conquests of other states in Nigeria described the Igbo as being the "most troublesome" group. One of the reasons why Igbo resistance was so difficult to confront was precisely because of this decentralized form of leadership, which meant that subduing the Igbo people would not have been as simple as merely conquering a centralized Igbo kingdom or subduing a particular Igbo ruler.

The decentralized nature of Igbo social organization was in direct contrast with the manner in which the colonial system was set up in British colonies. Under British colonial rule—which was a system of "indirect rule"—the colonial system was often upheld indirectly through the use of local rulers. Since the Igbo people were a decentralized group who were usually governed by village assemblies which were ran by elders, the British resorted to appointing chiefs to represent British policies.

The case of the Igbo people is also cited here because of the violence which was inflicted against the Igbo people when Nigeria became independent and because of the civil war which followed in 1967. Toyin Falola stated that: "Colonial rule restricted the economy and policies in a way that made competition inevitable. Power struggles and contests over land and boundaries added to the incidence of violence. The politics of managing local areas created tensions among chiefs and between communities." Colonial rule helped to create the conditions which would eventually lead to such extreme levels of violence in post-colonial Nigeria.

The leadership in post-colonial societies continued to engage in the same type of violent force which the colonial powers relied on. This was seen in Nigeria with the various military regimes which would run the country after independence came. This violence was also combined with a particular type of incompetence, which was so absurd and at times bizarre that it was almost humorous. Rodney stated in his speech: "Nowhere in the world do you find a scenario of politics to compare with some African and Caribbean states. One could write a scenario that is a sheer tragedy and one could write a scenario that is a comedy, and they would both be applicable."

Rodney spoke of the situation in Uganda, where someone like Idi Amin who was both a buffoon and a murderer could be the president of the country. This was the sort of situation which was seen throughout the post-colonial world to varying degrees. Political leaders could be incompetent and ineffective buffoons with an unsatiable desire for adulation, which was often taken to laughably absurd levels, yet those same leaders also often engaged in the murder and torture of their own population.

In Togo under Gnassingbé Eyadéma, citizens were made to line up to clap for him four times during the day, including when he was on his lunch break. Those who were caught not clapping for him were arrested. Civil servants were also made to wear uniforms with his image on it and to dance for him. The absurdity of this would almost be humorous if not for the tortures and killings which the Togolese people had to endure simply to appease the ego of Eyadéma. This was the type of scenario which confronted post-colonial societies. These were societies run by the likes of Gnassingbé Eyadéma and Idi Amin, and "Papa Doc" in Haiti and Mobutu in the Congo, which Mobutu had renamed to Zaire.

Independence for these colonial societies coincided with the Cold War, which was a struggle between the United States and the Soviet Union. One of the main features of this struggle was the ideological clash between the capitalism of the United States and the socialism of the Soviet Union. As African and Caribbean countries gained independence, they were also wrestling with whether to adopt capitalism or Marxism. This same question was also confronting Africans in the United States, who were beginning to question the entire capitalistic structure of the United States and who were paying close attention to the Marxist revolutions which were being carried out in other parts of the world, particularly in Cuba and in China.

One of the problems that Africans ran into was that white socialists still retained some of the racist attitudes of the dominant society. Assata Shakur explained that she began thinking of herself as a socialist, but she could not join any of the socialist groups which she came into contact with. She explained that she could not "stand the condescending, paternalistic attitudes of some of the white people in those groups." She also explained that she "couldn't relate to the idea of the great white father on earth any more than [I] could relate to the great white father up in the sky."

Africans who were engaged in the socialist struggle against capitalism had to confront the fact that the theories of Karl Marx were developed in Europe by a European man. This created the feeling that, as Shakur explained, Europeans "had a monopoly on Marx and acted like the only experts in the world on socialism came from Europe." For this reason, it was important for African socialists to be able to look to Third World revolutionary leaders who had embraced socialism. Shakur gave the examples of Fidel Castro, Ho Chi Minh, and Agostinho Neto as Third World revolutionaries who made contributions to the revolutionary socialist movement. Mao Tse-tung of China was another such individual.

Mao represented a non-white revolutionary who engaged in a successful revolution. Not only did this demonstrate that Europeans did not have a monopoly on Marxism, but it also created a sense of global solidarity among the non-white peoples of the world.

The Bandung Conference, which was held in 1955, was a conference which was attended by African and Asian nations. Malcolm X spoke about this conference in his "Ballot or the Bullet" speech. Malcolm explained that those who attended the conference had differences, such as religious differences. Despite this, the thing that united them was that they were not white. Malcolm explained: "The number-one thing that was not allowed to attend the Bandung conference was the white man. He couldn't come. Once they excluded the white man, they found that they could get together. Once they kept him out, everybody else fell right in and fell in line." Malcolm also explained: "They realized all over the world where the dark man was being oppressed, he was being oppressed by the white man; where the dark man was being exploited, he was being exploited by the white man. So they got together on this basis—that they had a common enemy."

Malcolm expressed the view that whenever white people were engaged in a revolution, that revolution was fought on the basis of white nationalism. Malcolm explained: "The American Revolution was white nationalism. The French Revolution was white nationalism. The Russian Revolution too — yes, it was — white nationalism. You don't think so? Why do you think Khrushchev and Mao can't get their heads together? White nationalism." Here Malcolm was expressing the view that whenever white people engaged in a revolution, it was done on the basis of asserting white interests and that Russia was no different.

In an interview with Robert Penn, Malcolm pointed out that he preferred Mao's approach over the more passive approach of Jawaharlal Nehru, who was India's first prime minister. Malcolm explained: "I think that Nehru brought his country up in a beggar's role. Their roles, the role of India and its reliance upon the West during the years since it got its supposed independence, has it today just as helpless and dependent as it was when it first got its independence. Whereas in China, the Chinese fought for their independence. They became militant right from the outstart, and today they're—even though they aren't loved, they are, they are respected. Though the West doesn't love them, the West respects them. Now, the West doesn't respect India, but it loves India."

Malcolm also used China's international strength as an example to demonstrate his view that Africa's independence would help to increase the respect accorded to African Americans. Malcolm explained: "The Chinese used to be disrespected. They used to use that expression in this country: 'You don't have a Chinaman's chance.' You remember that? You don't hear it lately. Because a Chinaman's got more chance than they have now. Why? Because China is strong. Since China became strong and independent, she's respected, she's recognized. So wherever a Chinese person goes, he is respected and he is recognized."

China was not the only Asian nation which Malcolm made reference to. Malcolm explained of the Japanese: "The Japanese on some of those islands in the Pacific, when the American soldiers landed, one Japanese sometimes could hold the whole army off. He'd just wait until the sun went down, and when the sun went down they were all equal. He would take his little blade and slip from bush to bush, and from American to American. The white soldiers couldn't cope with that." In the same speech, Malcolm also referred to the defeat of the French in French Indochina. He explained: "People who just a few years previously were rice farmers got together and ran the heavily-mechanized French army out of Indochina."

Malcolm saw the struggles of African Americans as part of a larger international struggle against Western hegemony and aggression towards the non-white people of the world. He looked to the struggles which Asian people were engaged in as a source of inspiration. He was not the only African to look to China. The Black Panther Party, which adopted the ideology of Marxism-Leninism, looked to Mao as a source of ideological inspiration. Mao appealed to African people not only racially because he was a non-white revolutionary leader, but also ideologically because Mao's revolution was a Marxist inspired revolution which sought to overthrow the capitalist system which was exploiting people throughout the world.

Africa would soon come to find that China's foreign policy towards African people was mostly strategic, rather than being rooted in a genuine desire to assist the revolutionary liberation struggle in Africa. This can be understood by the split between China and the Soviet Union, which was noted above.

This split led China to position itself against the Soviet Union in Africa. For example, Chinese Representative Lai Ya-li spoke before the United Nations General Assembly in 1975. His address was printed in the *Peking Review* and published on December 21, 1975. He used this opportunity to denounce the Soviet involvement in Angola, stating: "However, despite the termination of the Portuguese colonial rule, it has not been possible to form a government of national unity, and an unfortunate situation of division and civil war has emerged in Angola after independence. This is entirely the result of the contention between the two superpowers, and particularly the undisguised explosion and crude interference by that superpower which flaunts the signboard of 'socialism.'" He continued to state: "It is intolerable that the Soviet Union has carried out sabotage by every conceivable means and has even come out undisguisedly with repeated efforts to intimidate and exert pressure on some African countries. Obviously, the spearhead of the Soviet Union is directed not only against individual African countries, but against the O.A.U. and the African people as a whole. Such acts on the part of the Soviet Union have evoked the antipathy and indignation of many African countries and the broad masses of the African people. We resolutely condemn Soviet social-imperialism for its hegemonic acts of hostility towards Africa."

Lai Ya-li stated further: "The Soviet Union harbours ulterior motives in its wanton sabotage of the liberation cause of the Angolan people. [...] [T]he Soviet Union has set its mind on placing Angola under its control and turning it into an important stronghold in its rivalry with the other superpower over southern Africa and for command of the south Atlantic. Moreover, it has long cast a covetous eye on the abundant resources of Angola, anxious to have a hand in their plunder."

Although Lai Ya-li made references to the United States, the bulk of the criticism was directed at the Soviet Union. Ya-li even went so far as to charge the Soviet Union of "splitting the Angolan liberation organizations" as part of the plot to further divide Africa. Ya-li made no mention of the role that the apartheid state of South Africa played in fueling division between the differing organizations in Angola. In fact, China and South Africa supported the same side of the division. Both provided support for UNITA, which was a rival organization to the Soviet supported People's Movement for the Liberation of Angola.

In January 1973, China hosted Mobutu Sese Seko of Zaire. Mobutu came to power in a Western backed coup following the assassination of Patrice Lumumba. China had only recently normalized its relationship with Zaire in November of the previous year. The revolutionary government of China found itself hosting one of the most brutal and reactionary dictatorships in Africa. China's opposition to the Soviet Union placed China in a position where it was essentially adopting a pro-Western position in

Africa by supporting regimes in Africa which the Soviet Union was opposed to.

What is important to note here is that Malcolm had been very critical of the role that the United States played in the assassination of Lumumba and the destabilization of the Congo. By inviting Mobutu to China, the government of China demonstrated that it was not only willing to recognize the government of Mobutu, who played a role in overthrowing Lumumba, but that it was willing to also establish close diplomatic ties to Mobutu's dictatorship.

China's foreign policy in Africa demonstrated the limits of the Afro-Asian unity which Malcolm had spoken about. It is clear that Malcolm retained a great deal of respect for Mao and revolutionary China. He saw China as part of the global movement for liberation on the part of the non-white people of the world. The problem was that the politics of the Cold War was such that positioning itself against the Soviet Union became a greater concern for China than non-white solidarity against global European imperialism.

Here we see that the vision for a working class unity which cuts across racial identity was not to be found among Marxists in part because Marxists themselves were divided based on interpretations of Marxism, as well as the racial chauvinism of some of the white Marxists. There was yet another challenge which confronted the socialist ideology within the African struggle, however. It was not only that white Marxists and Chinese Maoists were willing to betray the principles of socialism where African people were concerned, but that even some of the African leaders who purported to be socialists were themselves not very much concerned with the principles of socialism.

In "Crisis in the Periphery: Africa and the Caribbean," Rodney addressed the issue of which class was to devise and implement the program for change. He explained that in African and Caribbean societies there were two components which had power. The first of which were the working people, whose power came from their production, although in most cases this was a potential power which was yet to be actualized. The other group with power was the group which controlled the state. This group controlled the allocation of resources and the allocation of surplus in the society. The latter group Rodney referred to as the petty (or petit) bourgeoisie—this was the class to which Rodney himself belonged to. Thomas Sankara, the former president of Burkina Faso, had described the petty bourgeoisie as a class which "often vacillates between the cause of the popular masses and that of imperialism. In its large majority, it always ends up by taking the side of the popular masses."

In Rodney's view, the working class should be the leading social group in the struggle. In his view, the petty bourgeoisie as a class is unable to lead a country anywhere except to destruction since that class was spawned from imperialism and capitalism within colonial societies. Rodney also rejected the socialist ideologies which were espoused by leaders who belonged to the petty bourgeoisie class.

Rodney's position was that the socialist ideologies of Kwame Nkrumah, Sékou Touré, Julius Nyerere, and Michael Manley did not go far enough in transforming social relations in post-colonial societies because these leaders had already established the hegemony of the petty bourgeoisie over the working class. Of the four men, I will place particular focus on Touré since he best exemplifies the particular contradictions which Walter Rodney was speaking about.

One particular problem with Touré's approach in Guinea was that it was undemocratic. Walter Rodney pointed out that in post-colonial Africa, many leaders rejected democracy. Rodney explained that these leaders had taken a specific type of "bourgeois democracy" and presented it as the absolute form of democracy, thereby rejecting the entire concept. Instead, these states adopted a "species of authoritarianism" in which working people were effectively unable to make choices within the society.

Some African leaders argued that having a single-state party was necessary because having too many parties could create division. President Joseph Momoh of Sierra Leone explained: "As your president, I have to say it loud and clear—multi-partyism at this point of our social and economic development will only spell doom for us and take us right back to those old dangerous days of divisiveness, conflict, victimisation and vindictiveness that we have happily left behind for well over a decade." He also added that "the principle and practice of the system of popular participation under the one-party democracy over the years has proved to be very useful." In Cameroon, Paul Biya denounced the demands for multiple parties as a diversion from the country's economic crisis. He also applauded party loyalists for organizing pro-government demonstrations.

In some cases, regimes which established one-party rule even called themselves democratic. Sékou Touré's party in Guinea was known as the Democratic Party of Guinea. The suppression of certain rights and the abuses which took place under Touré's rule was justified as being necessary to protect the revolution in Guinea from imperialist forces. There is no denying that there were imperialist forces who were seeking to overthrow the government of Guinea, as had been done to Nkrumah in Ghana. The problem was that in the end, despite the use of brutal force against Guinean citizens, the regime in Guinea ultimately ended up adopting a position which was pro-Western and pro-capitalist. As I explained in *Malcolm X, Bob Marley, and Other Essays*, Guinea moved towards production for the benefit of capitalist economies.

As Rodney pointed out, the "choice of production" in post-colonial societies was determined not within those societies themselves, but by the "metropolitan core economies." The pattern of production in post-colonial societies remained exporting products which those societies themselves do not consume. This is what was done in Guinea at the expense of the working people. The socialism which many post-colonial leaders preached did not bring about a significant transformation in this system of production.

The Fifth Pan-African Congress represented a shift towards a more class conscious approach. This shift can be seen in W.E.B. Du Bois' own ideological growth. Du Bois, who was an organizer in the previous four congresses, had favored what he called the "Talented Tenth." He described his belief as follows in *Dusk of Dawn*: "I believed in the higher education of a Talented Tenth who through their knowledge of modem culture could guide the American Negro into a higher civilization. I knew that without this the Negro would have to accept white leadership, and that such leadership could not always be trusted to guide this group into self-realization and to its highest cultural possibilities."

Du Bois had expressed the view that "the power of this aristocracy of talent was to lie in its knowledge and character and not in its wealth." In *Souls of Black Folk*, Du Bois had expressed the view that the "worker must work for the glory of his handiwork, not simply for pay; the thinker must think for truth, not for fame." Du Bois was not someone who expressed the view that leadership should be determined by wealth or that individuals should be driven by wealth and fame, but at this particular point Du Bois also was not very conscious of class relations. In time Du Bois would critique his earlier vision of the Talented Tenth, explaining: "The problem which I did not then attack was that of leadership and authority within the group, which by implication left controls to wealth—a contingency of which I never dreamed. But now the whole economic trend of the world has changed. That mass and class must unite for the world's salvation is clear. We who have had least class differentiation in wealth, can follow in the new trend and indeed lead it."

Nkrumah served as the joint secretary to the Fifth Pan-African Congress along with George Padmore, a Trinidadian—Du Bois attended this congress as well. One of the declarations at this Congress stated: "The Fifth Pan-African Congress calls on intellectuals and professional classes of the Colonies to awaken to their responsibilities. The long, long night is over. By fighting for trade union rights, the right to form co-operatives, freedom of the press, assembly, demonstration and strike, freedom to print and read the literature which is necessary for the education of the masses, you will be using the only means by which your liberties will be won and maintained. Today there is only one road to effective action—the organization of the masses."

Nkrumah explained in *Africa Must Unite*: "Unlike the first four Congresses, which had been supported mainly by middle-class intellectuals and bourgeois reformists, the Fifth Pan-African Congress was attended by workers, trade unionists, farmers and students, most of whom came from Africa." In *The Intellectual and Political Legacy of Walter Rodney* I pointed to Walter Rodney's criticism of the "vanguard" of the Fifth Pan-African Congress, which Rodney claims lost its direction and began to engage in bourgeois theory.

In "Marx in the Liberation of Africa," Rodney argued that for "years Nkrumah went along with this mish-mash of philosophy which took some socialist premises but in which he refused to pursue to their logical conclusion—that one either had a capitalist system based upon the private ownership of the means of production and the alienation of the product of people's labour or one had an alternative system which was completely different and that there was no way of juxtaposing and mixing these two to create anything that was new and viable." After Nkrumah was overthrown, he went to Guinea where he wrote *Class Struggle in Africa*. Rodney explained that the importance of this book is that in this book Nkrumah "admits the consequences, the misleading consequences of an ideology which espoused an African cause, but which felt, for reasons which he did not understand, a historical necessity to separate itself from Scientific Socialism."

In Rodney's view, the advancement of post-colonial societies could only be carried out through the efforts of the working class and that if the petty bourgeoisie as a class was to have a role in this process it would be to shift the initiative into the hands of workers and peasants, and then to serve those classes, rather than serving the capitalist class.

I quote Sankara again, who explained that "the educated petty bourgeoisie of Africa—if not the Third World—is not prepared to give up its privileges, either due to intellectual laziness or simply because it has tasted the Western way of life." For this reason, the petty bourgeoisie often became an obstacle in the way of genuine liberation.

Apart from developing an ideological approach to address the exploitation and class differences produced by colonialism in Africa, there were also internal class developments within African society that must be explored in order to understand the developments which took place within post-colonial society. This was something which Amilcar Cabral confronted in his struggle to liberate Guinea-Bissau and Cape Verde from Portuguese colonial rule. He not only had to contend with the hierarchy which was established by Portuguese colonial domination in Guinea-Bissau and Cape Verde, but also internal class relationships within pre-colonial African societies.

Among those who preached African Socialism, which was yet another brand of petty bourgeois socialism, there was a view that the concept of class was alien to African societies, which was far from reality. It is certainly true that capitalism did not develop in Africa and African societies avoided the type of harsh feudalism which was practiced in Europe, but this does not mean that there were no class distinctions within pre-colonial African society. In their colonial conquests, Europeans often attempted to exploit existing class distinctions. The Igbo people were cited earlier as an example where Europeans resorted to creating a class hierarchy for the purpose of entrenching indirect colonial rule through selected chiefs.

Cabral addressed the pre-colonial class structure in Guinea-Bissau, which was not uniformly developed. The Balanta people developed what Cabral called "a horizontal society," which meant that there were no classes above another. There were no great chiefs until the Portuguese arrived and made chiefs for the Balanta people. Regarding the individual accumulation of wealth, Cabral stated: "Balanta society is like this: the more land you work, the richer you are, but the wealth is not to be hoarded, it is to be spent, for one individual cannot be much more than another."

Cabral explained that others had vertical societies, in which there was a chief at the top. The chiefs along with religious leaders formed what Cabral called a class. Then there were professionals such as clobbers, blacksmiths, and goldsmiths who did not have the same rights as those at the top. Cabral explained that by tradition, "anyone who was a goldsmith was even ashamed of it—all the more if he were a 'griot' (minstrel)."

Below the professionals there were those who tilled the ground. The tillers tilled the ground for the chiefs. Cabral explained that in Fula and Manjaco society, chiefs were linked to God and for this reason held authority over the tillers. Among the Majaco people, a tiller could not till without the chief's order.

Cabral noted that the nature of Fula society was structured to maintain this class hierarchy, but this is not to suggest that there were not conflicts. Cabral explained that there have been major peasant uprisings among the Fula people. In one instance, Mussa Molo overthrew a king and took the king's place. Cabral noted that this overthrow did not result in a significant structural change because Mussa Molo kept the same laws in place.

Cabral was forced to confront contradictions between ethnic groups, which were displayed not only in terms of different social structures among the various ethnic groups, but also in terms of prior military conflicts among the ethnic groups. Cabral explained that the Fula and Mandinga, unlike the Balanta, had chiefs. Cabral also explained that the majority of Fula and Mandinga in Guinea-Bissau were persons who became Mandinga and Fula. Cabral spoke of individuals being "Mandingized" as a result of Mandingo conquests.

The expansion of kingdoms resulted in wars and conquests in which certain conquered groups became absorbed into the dominant group. Wars and conflicts of this nature were an aspect of Africa's own internal development, but such conflicts were used by the Portuguese to provoke divisions among the people as part of the colonial divide and conquer tactic which kept Africans divided among each other thereby making it easier for Europeans to conquer and subjugate African people. Cabral sought to unite the society around chasing out the Portuguese colonizers.

Cabral also sought to unify the three classes in his society: the ruling class, the artisan class, and the peasant class. He recognized that this did not mean that everyone had to be united. In fact, Cabral acknowledged that there were certain self-interested individuals who "are afraid of losing their privileges in favour of the struggle."

I cite Cabral because he was an anti-colonial leader in Africa who attempted to wrestle not only with class relations which were produced by European colonialism, but also with the pre-existing class structures within traditional African societies and how those existing contradictions hindered the struggle against Portuguese colonialism.

The end of colonialism in Africa and the Caribbean did not bring about the type of fundamental transformations which were needed. Many of the post-colonial leaders retained the same basic features of the colonial society, which was a society in which the working class remained poor and exploited, while laboring for the benefit of wealthy capitalist nations. The significance of Walter Rodney's assessment of post-colonial society is that he understood this transformation could only come from the workers and the peasants, who made up the masses of the post-colonial society, and who were also the most neglected and exploited segment of post-colonial society.